For my wife and family. I love you all very much and thank you for your constant support, and if you ever considered not believing in me, I appreciate that you were nice enough to never let me know.

First Montag Press E-Book and Paperback Original Edition October 2014

Montag Press
ISBN: 978-1-940233-12-3
Cover art, layout, & e-book © 2014 Rick Febré
Author photo © 2014 Kathleen Keller

Montag Press Team:
Project Editor – Charlie Franco
Managing Director – Charlie Franco

A Montag Press Book
www.montagpress.com
Montag Press
536 E. 8th Street
Davis CA, 95616 USA

Montag Press, the burning book with the hatchet cover, the skewed word mark and the portrayal of the long-suffering fireman mascot are trademarks of Montag Press.

Printed & Digitally Originated in the United States of America
10 9 8 7 6 5 4 3 2 1

THE END OF JACK CRUZ

BY DAVID L. WILLIAMS

ADAPTED FROM THE NOVEL BY A.A. GARRISON

MONTAG

THE END OF JACK CRUZ

BY DAVID L. WILLIAMS

ADAPTED FROM THE NOVEL BY A.A. GARRISON

CAST OF CHARACTERS

COLONEL
Jack Jones, former junkie.

CRUZ
Jack Cruz, a bald, muscular, former psych professor.

MACY
Jack Macy, an older survivor of The Slick.

GWEN
Gwen Lander, a female survivor of The Slick.

PLACE

A food processing warehouse. At center is a kitchen table and light kitchen set-up. Downstage right are cots. Stage left has an exit to Cruz's lab. Stage right has a door and window to the outside.

Act I

Lights up on a warehouse. JACK CRUZ, a man of average height but full of muscles, massive with a bald head, enters. HE walks with purpose across the room, carrying a gym bag. COLONEL, a tall, skinny man enters as CRUZ did, but HE is unsure of his surroundings. CRUZ exits and then the sound of a generator STARTING. The lights flicker on. COLONEL takes a look at the place. CRUZ enters and walks past COLONEL who is about to say something, but refrains. CRUZ takes a padlock from his pocket, puts it on the door, and locks it.

COLONEL
Hey, um ... listen ...

> *(But HE trails off when CRUZ walks toward him. CRUZ takes a key off of his key chain and puts it in COLONEL's hand. CRUZ speaks with an Aussie accent.)*

CRUZ
To keep riff-raff out. Not us in.

COLONEL
Right.

(CRUZ puts the gym bag on the table and sits down, rummaging through it.)

I guess I should thank you.

CRUZ
You guess?

COLONEL
For back at the hospital. For saving my life.

CRUZ
Uh-huh.

COLONEL
It was, um ... I wasn't in the greatest shape.

CRUZ
How long had it been?

COLONEL
I don't know. A week, ten days maybe. Probably.

CRUZ
The Germ does tend to scramble one's brains.

COLONEL
That's what you call it, huh? The Germ? That's good. I like that better than "The Slick." Yeah, you get sweaty. Who gives a shit? The Vomit, or The fuckin' Moan. That's what they should've fuckin' called the disease.

CRUZ
While you're here, and you may feel free to stay as long as you like, I won't ask for much, but as a religious man, I'd appreciate if you toned down your language.

COLONEL
Oh. Sorry.

CRUZ
No need. You didn't know.

COLONEL
(Awkward pause, then)
You're still religious after all this? Or I guess this could make a guy more religious.

CRUZ
Plagues are a common feature in the Good Book.

COLONEL
Yeah. Anyways, thank you. Thank you for saving my life. It's mighty Christian of you. Or Jewish, or Muslim, or whatever you are.

CRUZ
You were right the first time. I worship our lord and savior, Jesus Christ.

COLONEL
Great. That's ... great.
(Awkward pause. CRUZ takes a good deal of

*pharmaceuticals out of the bag and starts dividing them
into two piles on the table.)*

COLONEL *(cont'd)*
What, um ... sorry.

CRUZ
(Not looking at him)
Go ahead. I can do two things at once, sir.

COLONEL
Colonel. Everybody calls me Colonel.

CRUZ
In what branch of the armed forces did you serve?

COLONEL
No, I, it's a nickname. I went as a soldier one
Halloween and— They have Halloween where you're
from?

CRUZ
I'm familiar with the holiday.

COLONEL
Right. Kids started calling me Colonel that day
and it just stuck. Jack Jones if you need it for legal
documents, but I don't think it much matters anymore.

CRUZ
Coincidences abound, Colonel. Jack Jones, Jack Cruz.

COLONEL *(Shaking hands with him)*
Nice to meet you, Jack. Two Jacks, huh? Get three
ladies in here and we'll have a pretty good hand, right?

(Realizing)

No offense to your religious beliefs or whatnot.

(Awkward pause)

You mind me asking, why did you pick me?

CRUZ
Why did I *pick* you?

COLONEL
That other fella had a gun on me and I had a spike in
my arm. In a pinch, I might've taken the guy who knew
how to handle himself in a scuffle and not some junkie
with the Slick, the Germ.

CRUZ
You were taking the medicine to fend off the Germ,
yes?

COLONEL
Sure.

CRUZ
And that man with the gun, he wanted to take all the
medicine you had? I'll choose a man of peace, a man
who wants to be left alone, over a common thief any day.

COLONEL
All right then. I'm glad you did. Though, shooting him

through the eye was a little—

CRUZ

(Indicating the piles)

This is your share, Colonel, and this is mine.

*(HE turns the bag over to show that
it's empty.)*

You'll agree these are even piles? I haven't cheated you.

COLONEL

Of course. You've been very generous.

CRUZ

Not generous, but fair. If we're to reside together, and
that is completely up to you, then my only demand is a
fair house. Is that square with you, Colonel?

COLONEL

Absolutely, Jack.

CRUZ

Good. There are several footlockers here. You may avail
yourself to any of them.

COLONEL

Okay.

*(CRUZ sweeps his drugs into the bag.
HE picks it up and begins to walk away.)*

Where do you keep yours?

CRUZ
Colonel, there are certain things I wish to—

COLONEL
No, no, no. I just, I thought maybe you could keep mine in there with yours. I could get on your schedule of fixing, keeping the sickness away. You seem like a solid guy, Cruz, and I've got a bad habit of losing things.

CRUZ
If that's what you'd prefer.

COLONEL
I would. I really would.

CRUZ
All right then. I shall serve as apothecary.

> *(HE sweeps the rest of the drugs into the bag as well and then exits. COLONEL walks around the warehouse and checks it out. There are a few cots and then HE notices a bucket full of hundred dollar bills. CRUZ returns.)*

COLONEL
I didn't know I was saved by a rich guy. You saving this for when the world gets back on its feet?

CRUZ
It's an effective toilet paper.

COLONEL
I bet it is.

CRUZ
You called yourself a junkie before.

COLONEL
I'm not the first person to call me that.

CRUZ
If it's out of necessity, though, not recreational—

COLONEL
It can't be both?

CRUZ
So you were an addict before the Germ.

COLONEL
In recovery, swear to Chr— I promise. But when the Slick got me and I was on death's door, I figured, go with a smile, right? Took the last stash I had hidden just in case, and I felt better. A hundred percent better. Getting the Slick, it's like going cold turkey, isn't it?

CRUZ
The symptoms of the virus do, indeed, appear to be remarkably similar to the signs of opiate withdrawal. Having never gone through them myself, I had to study the disease to make these connections. I'm not a doctor, no, but I do have some medical training.

COLONEL
You're a lucky man. When I got to Nevada State I had to got through all of the withdrawal bullshit, B.S., sorry. It was no fun.

CRUZ
This is university?

COLONEL
Nevada State Penitentiary.

CRUZ
You're a felon?

COLONEL
I was trying to sell some drugs, make a big score so I could ... anyway, they gave me a couple of years. I got out a year or so ago. Just in time to watch the world end.
          (Slight pause, then)
Probably not what you wanted to hear about your new roommate, huh?
          (Silence. CRUZ takes a couple of
          cans from the kitchen area.)

CRUZ
Hungry?

COLONEL
Absolutely.
          (CRUZ tosses a can to COLONEL, who

*opens it. HE takes a pocket knife
from his pocket and eats peaches in
syrup with his knife. CRUZ takes a
fork from the kitchen area and does
the same.)*

So what do you do around here, Jack?

CRUZ
I'm trying to research the Germ, unlock its secrets,
maybe even find a cure beyond this amelioration. On
occasion I will go out to hunt for supplies.

COLONEL
And I'm glad you did today.

(A bite of peaches, then)

You mind if I go out with you next time?

CRUZ
We'll see. Why don't you take a few days to get
acclimated to Stevens before we start making grand
plans.

COLONEL
This place belonged to a friend of yours?

CRUZ
What?

COLONEL
This Steven guy? Did you know him?

CRUZ

Stevens Foods. You're in a warehouse, Colonel.

(HE walks over and grabs the bucket of cash.)

Make yourself at home. Get some sleep.
If you'll excuse me.

COLONEL

Sure, Cruz.

*(CRUZ exits. COLONEL finishes up his
peaches and then goes over to a cot.
HE collapses into it, and gets under
the covers. HE tries to get comfortable,
kicking out the military corners on
the well-made bed. When HE finally
does, HE realizes that something is on
his foot. HE reaches into the covers
and comes out with a pair of women's
underwear. HE looks at it, the puts it
under his pillow. And then the sound of
a sistrum (an ancient Egyptian musical
instrument) three times. This isn't
diegetic, it is simply the eerie sound
of time passing. With the sound of the
sistrum comes a brief blackout/ light
flicker, three seconds or so. COLONEL
gets up and starts stretching. CRUZ
enters. HE goes and retrieves a bottle
of water without comment.)*

COLONEL

How are things in the lab?

CRUZ
How are *things*?

COLONEL
Sure. Come up with a cure yet?

CRUZ
No. Medicine will just have to do for now.

COLONEL
I'm ... I'm nothing to be afraid of.

CRUZ
Excuse me?

COLONEL
You haven't come out of your lab in a couple days, and
I figured it's because of me being here and—

CRUZ
I come out everyday.

COLONEL
Well, yesterday I didn't see you, so I—

CRUZ
You were asleep when I came out. That's the first time.
The second time I didn't see you either.

COLONEL
Oh. I was ... I was outside at that point, I guess.
Getting fresh air. Or slightly less stale air, anyway.

CRUZ

I'm sorry the accommodations aren't up to your high standards, Colonel, but they suit my simple tastes just fine.

COLONEL

That's not what I was saying.

CRUZ

And I apologize that I haven't adapted to your schedule yet, but I prefer to relax at night when you chose to sleep.

COLONEL

I didn't mean to get you pissed off at me, I—

(Off his look)

That word's on the list too, huh? I didn't mean to get you *angry* at me. I just ... I feel like me being a junky, a former junky, may have freaked you out a little.

CRUZ

Ah.

COLONEL

And I understand. Believe me, I do. We don't have the best reputation for good reason. You didn't know that about me when you picked me up. Maybe you would've left me if you had known, but it's too late now. Me here, having to use every few days to stay alive ... I'm saying, I'd be worried if I moved in with me.

CRUZ
(Slight pause) So what do I do?

COLONEL
Yeah.

CRUZ
How do I have you live here without any concern?

COLONEL
Well, if you're worried about a fight ... you're not
worried about a fight. You got all the muscles in the
world. You know, you probably do have all the muscles
in the world at this point.

CRUZ
There are still weapons.

COLONEL
I don't like 'em. I don't even like my bread knife to be
too sharp.

CRUZ
And if I don't believe you?

COLONEL
You could always carry something on you.

> *(CRUZ takes a gun out from behind*
> *him and puts it on the table in*
> *front of him, never taking his*
> *hand off of it.)*

Like the biggest gun ever made, for example.
You want to give me random pat-downs, all that, it's
fine. I'm a peaceful guy.

CRUZ
You're an ex-con.

COLONEL
For selling drugs. Nothing violent.

CRUZ
Incarceration changes a man. From what I hear.

COLONEL
Yeah. It taught me to knock off the drugs so I never go
back to that shithole ever again. Sorry, craphole, or
feceshole, or whatever.

(Silence)

I could go. If you're not happy having me here, I
understand it. You can give me my half of the medicine
and I'll be out of your life forever. But I'd like to stay, if
you'll have me.

CRUZ
I'm not so—

COLONEL
Being alone makes you do crazy things. Having
somebody else around, it reminds you that you're
human.

CRUZ
You believe that to be true?

COLONEL
I've seen it. Guys came back from solitary and they weren't the same. As loud and awful as prison was, I didn't ever want to be alone.

CRUZ *(A slight pause, then)*
Would you be willing to help me with my work?

COLONEL
Finding a cure? Absolutely.

CRUZ
It may involve tedious tasks like searching abandoned stores for a list of ingredients. It may take days to find just one tincture.

COLONEL
I think I can clear my schedule for that. Whatever you need, Cruz.

> *(CRUZ picks up his gun and puts*
> *it back into his waist. HE opens*
> *the bottle of water and takes a*
> *long drink.)*

CRUZ
Do you know the story of Cain and Abel, Colonel?

COLONEL
Brothers who didn't get along? That's not something
you need to worry about—

CRUZ *(Waving him off)*
I'm not trying to express something metaphorically.
I'm talking about the actual story from the holy
scripture.

COLONEL
One of them killed the other. That's about all I know.

CRUZ
Cain slew Abel out of jealousy. Abel kept the flocks and
Cain tended the fields. Abel had to fight off wolves that
came after his sheep, and Cain had to plant lentils.
Of the two of us, which one seems more like a wolf-
fighter and which seems more like a lentil-planter?

> *(No answer)*

And yet Cain was able to rise up and slay Abel.
Sometimes muscles don't mean a thing. I believe one of
your presidents said, "Trust but verify." Those will be
my watch words.

> *(HE motions for COLONEL to assume
> the position. COLONEL does so.
> CRUZ pats him down, somewhat
> aggressively and definitely thoroughly.
> Finding nothing, HE lets him go.)*

I'll need some supplies for my research. You'll go and
hunt for them tomorrow?

COLONEL
Whatever you need, Cruz. I'm your guy.

CRUZ
I'll make a list.
> *(HE finishes his bottled water and
> exits. COLONEL watches him go. HE
> finishes one last stretch and then
> takes a jog around the warehouse.
> HE runs off stage. The sound of the
> sistrum. CRUZ enters and puts a
> kit of medicine and syringe on the
> table. A banging on the door.
> CRUZ gets up and unlocks the padlock.
> COLONEL comes in with a duffel bag
> and sees a dazed CRUZ, head nodding a
> bit, a smile on his face for the first
> time.)*

CRUZ
Colonel!

COLONEL
You started without me.

CRUZ
When I need I take it. I try to set aside ritual for fear I
become addicted to the regularity of it.

COLONEL
That's not what I was addicted to.

CRUZ
What did you find?

COLONEL
What did I find? What you asked me to find.

CRUZ
I'm not my best self at the moment. Remind me.

COLONEL
Test tubes and dope.

CRUZ
The two great tastes that taste great together.

COLONEL
You really are fucked up, huh?

CRUZ
I'm gonna let that one go, so yes, probably.

COLONEL
I'll have to remember that.

CRUZ
How much did you get?

COLONEL
You think I could join you there, Cruz?

CRUZ
I want you to answer my question first.

COLONEL
Um, okay ... I've got a good haul. The retirement home
had a lot of dope, more than I thought they would. I
stopped by a physical therapy place too, but they—

CRUZ
Is that why you're late?

COLONEL
Am I on a schedule here?

CRUZ
I am. And when I have to depend on you for supplies,
then you are too. Had you followed my instructions, I
was expecting you an hour ago. That's why I gave you
instructions; for you to follow them. This explains why
I was mistaken.

COLONEL
I guess so.

CRUZ
The physical therapy business, they had no drugs. No
test tubes.

COLONEL
Didn't see any, no.

CRUZ
I'm not asking you, I'm telling you. They don't do
science there, they just do stretching. Or, they *did* do
that.

(CRUZ giggles at this.)

Now you may sit. Just careful where you put those test tubes.

COLONEL
All right.
> *(HE puts the bag down on a cot and
> then sits with CRUZ.)*

CRUZ
Are you a religious man, Colonel?

COLONEL
I'll pray to whatever I need to to make sure I survive.

CRUZ
That's not what I was asking. I wasn't looking for a glib answer.

COLONEL
Sorry.

CRUZ
So?

COLONEL
My mom taught me that talking about religion is the best way to ruin any relationship. She'd know, considering my dad divorced her after he found God, and a bunch of other women in his new church.

CRUZ
Then you and the Almighty don't have much of a relationship. That's understandable.

COLONEL
But whatever you need, Cruz. I don't judge.

CRUZ
Perhaps you haven't met the God I serve yet.

COLONEL
I've heard the, uh, the good news, heard it plenty.

CRUZ
That's Christ. God's a different beast. The Old Testament, God's half of the bible, that's a book of survival tactics. God keeps throwing natural disasters and invading armies at people and seeing the ones who survive. He builds nations out of the winners.

COLONEL
That's an interesting way to look at it.

CRUZ
We're survivors, you and I. We figured out how to live through this.

COLONEL
I just lucked into it. My bad habits helped me out.

> *(HE goes to reach for the syringe,*
> *but CRUZ pulls it away.)*

CRUZ

You're right. You were spared by the mercy of the
Almighty. But I didn't take poison into my veins
before all of this, before his wrath. I saw everyone
getting sick, even felt a sniffle or two of my own, and I
recognized that it wasn't the flu or anything as simple
as that. Plague. Recognizable plague. I took the tiniest
little bit, injected it between my toes, as far away from
my heart as I could get, and the next day

(HE snaps his fingers)

clean as a whistle. Clean as a holy saint. I figured it
out. God willed me to survive and I did. Perhaps he'll
make a great nation out of me.

*(HE gets up and pushes the syringe
and medicine to COLONEL. HE picks
up the bag and walks to the exit
but stops.)*

I'll be working with chemicals soon.

COLONEL

All right.

CRUZ

Volatile chemicals. No cure without them.

COLONEL

I'll be careful with whatever you need me to get.

CRUZ

You misunderstand me. A trend, I see.

COLONEL
Maybe if you were a little clearer.

CRUZ
Maybe if you let me finish a thought instead of
jumping in with your own.

    (Silence, then)

I'll be working with volatile chemicals, susceptible to
changes in air pressure, temperature, what have you. If
I'm in my lab, makeshift as it is, I can't just have you
breaking open the door to tell me any little thing. I'll
need my privacy. I trust that you won't take that as a
personal slight to you.

COLONEL
I'll knock before I—

CRUZ
You can knock all you like. I'm installing a lock. I'll
control when my door is open and when it's closed.
Are we clear?

COLONEL
Crystal.

CRUZ
Good. Enjoy your medicine.

        (CRUZ exits and COLONEL goes to
        the table. HE looks at the syringe
        and it's full. HE remembers something
        and exits the way he came in. The

sound of the sistrum. COLONEL enters
with a new duffel bag.)

COLONEL
Cruz, I'm back!

> *(HE puts the duffel bag on the*
> *table. CRUZ enters, looking*
> *clear-eyed, taking off a pair*
> *of gloves.)*

I'm not late, am I?

CRUZ
On the contrary. I wasn't expecting you for another
fifteen minutes.

COLONEL
I used to run track, back in high school, and now
there's a million places to run without getting
bothered. I wanna get back into running shape.

CRUZ
The chemicals I'm having you seek are—

COLONEL
I only—

> *(HE stops himself)*

No, sorry. You go. I've gotta stop doing that.

CRUZ
I would prefer you not run with them, for fear they
break, mix, degrade. Explode.

COLONEL *(Slight pause, then)*
Anything else?

CRUZ
I think I've made myself clear. Let's see what is
salvageable.

> *(HE goes and opens the duffel*

bag. HE is pleasantly surprised
at what he's found.)

COLONEL
All good, right? I was gonna tell you that I figured
you'd say that, about not running with them, so I ran
there and walked back.

CRUZ
Those were good decisions, Colonel. I salute you.

COLONEL
Well, you can't be both the brawn and the brains. I've
gotta contribute something.

CRUZ
The legs, perhaps. Thank you for this.

> *(HE takes the bag and goes to exit*
> *but COLONEL's voice stops him.)*

COLONEL
How does it work? The cure?

CRUZ
I haven't found one yet.

COLONEL
But when you do. I have faith in you.

CRUZ
Do you know how the opioid receptors in the brain work?

COLONEL
Not ... fully.

CRUZ
The use of buprenorphine as an epsilon antagonist?

COLONEL
Oh, I totally know what that is, sure. They teach that in second grade here.

CRUZ
There are hardly a dearth of books here, Colonel. You could pick one up and read once in a while, spend some time away from the handheld video games that suck up every battery you can squirrel away.

COLONEL
Maybe dumb it down a few degrees

CRUZ
You've dug holes in the sand at the beach? That's not beyond your experience, is it?

COLONEL
Sure, I've done that.

CRUZ
What happened to them?

COLONEL
Tide came in and filled them up with water.

CRUZ
And what if you had concrete to pour into those holes.

COLONEL
Then they'd be holes full of concrete.

CRUZ
No water would be able to get in.

COLONEL
So the Slick is the water?

CRUZ
And the receptors are the holes. We've been using drugs to fill the holes, but drugs aren't concrete. They get washed away. I'm trying to create concrete.

COLONEL
That makes sense.

CRUZ
Well, good, but it's a hundred times more complicated than that.

COLONEL
Sorry you have to keep explaining things to your stupid packhorse.

CRUZ
Ah.

(*Slight pause*)

You're feeling less than appreciated.

COLONEL
It's not that.

CRUZ
I do value the time it saves me for you to gather supplies, but it's—

COLONEL
I know you could do it yourself, Cruz. You've made it clear that you're multitalented, and all I'm saving you is time.

CRUZ
It's a crude way of putting it.

COLONEL
But it's time you'll have when you're cured. I'm not looking for thank you notes, but a little guidance beyond "go get this and go get that," that'd be appreciated.

CRUZ
Guidance how?

COLONEL
I don't know Jane Eyre from Air Bud. A reading list
would be nice.

CRUZ
You'd like that?

COLONEL
So I don't waste my time on books I don't need to read.

CRUZ
Time reading a book is never wasted time.

COLONEL
Oh yeah? Well, I saw some books about maximizing
earnings in the stock market today. Should I have
brought them back to you?

CRUZ
Fair point. I'll have a list for you tonight.

COLONEL
Thank you. Am I as demanding as your previous
assistant?

CRUZ
Excuse me?

COLONEL
My first night here, I found a pair of women's, um ...
unless they were yours, and if so we can stop having
this conversation right now.

CRUZ
Oh. No. They were Laura's.

COLONEL
Laura was your assistant or girlfriend or both maybe?

CRUZ
None of the above. She was a refugee from the
Sickness, like you. Not as dedicated to finding a cure,
though. She mainly wanted to lament about her family
that had succumbed. This was in the early days of the
plague.

COLONEL
Did she not want to take the medicine?

CRUZ
No, she ... Ah. You think she's dead.

COLONEL
Well, since she's not here—

CRUZ
She may be dead, I have no idea. She took off one
morning before I woke. She had been threatening to
go back to wherever she was from and bury her infant
child. I would assume she did that and didn't desire to
return.

COLONEL
Sorry.

CRUZ
We all must take the paths we feel are best and hope thatthe path we chose is the one that the Almighty desires for us.

COLONEL
Um, Amen. Sure.

CRUZ
Thank you for these, Colonel. I'll get to drawing up that reading list right now.

>   *(HE exits. COLONEL goes and gets*
>   *the underwear from below a pillow*
>   *and tosses it in their garbage*
>   *can. HE takes a fruit cup from*
>   *the fridge, opens it up, and starts*
>   *eating. HE exits as he does. The*
>   *sound of the sistrum. COLONEL enters*
>   *with a duffel bag over his shoulder,*
>   *reading **Leaves of Grass**. HE puts*
>   *the bag on the counter)*

COLONEL
Cruz, why was the door un—

>   *(HE stops when HE sees that SOMEONE*
>   *is sleeping in a cot. HE looks at*
>   *the man for a second, puzzled, and*
>   *then walks over to CRUZ's lab. HE*
>   *wants to knock on the door, but*
>   *hesitates. The MAN, JACK MACY, sits*
>   *up in bed as COLONEL considers*

interrupting Cruz, but HE is strapped
in there.)

MACY
Heyyyy! HEYYYYY!

> *(COLONEL drops his book. MACY hears*
> *this and tries to turn his head to*
> *see COLONEL, but can't.)*

Nurse! I gotta get up! Please!!

COLONEL
Um, um, one, one second.

MACY
Nurse, nurse, nurse!!

> *(COLONEL goes to knock on the lab*
> *door for real this time, but CRUZ*
> *comes out before HE can, holding a*
> *syringe.)*

COLONEL
He's, uh, that guy's awake.

CRUZ
I gathered.

COLONEL
He thinks he's in a hospital. He keeps calling for a—

MACY
NURSE!!

COLONEL
Nurse.

CRUZ
Thank you, Colonel.

COLONEL
Who is he?

CRUZ
You have to give him some medicine.

COLONEL
I do?

CRUZ
Yes. I'll be holding him down, so I can't—

MACY
NURSE!

CRUZ
    (Sharply)
The nurse will only come if you stop yelling.
    (To CRUZ)
As I was saying, I'll be—

COLONEL
I could hold him down. I mean, I'm not great at
injecting anybody but myself.

CRUZ
With your checkered past?

COLONEL
Maybe a couple of times, in a pinch, but—

CRUZ
Well, this is a pinch. I'm stronger than you, Colonel. If I hold him down, he'll stay down and you can inject him. If you hold him, he may get lose, knock the syringe out of my hand and into my eye. Or your eye.

COLONEL
(An exhale, then)
Fine.
(CRUZ hands him the syringe. THEY walk over to MACY.)

MACY
Doc, I'm sorry, I ... I went a little wild there. I'm not used to being strapped down like this. I get a little claustrophobic and—

CRUZ
Stop talking.
(MACY shuts up and CRUZ leans down and pins Macy's arms down. MACY freaks out even more at this, but CRUZ is insistent in keeping him down.)
Anytime, Colonel.

> *(COLONEL nods, finds a vein on*
> *MACY's arm and then injects him.*
> *HE goes halfway.)*

The whole syringe, please. He's in a state.

> *(COLONEL complies and MACY really*
> *feels the drugs. HE tries to say*
> *something, but HE's way too high*
> *to come up with anything more than*
> *some incoherent babbling. Even*
> *that goes away quickly and HE nods*
> *off, half-asleep, half in another*
> *world. COLONEL removes the syringe*
> *and CRUZ lets him go.)*

CRUZ
Good, thank you.

> *(CRUZ heads back to his lab and*
> *COLONEL stands there stunned.)*

COLONEL
Um ...

CRUZ
> *(Stopping)*
You have questions.

> *(COLONEL is getting sick of CRUZ's*
> *mysterious pretensions.)*

COLONEL
Yeah, a few.

CRUZ
Macy is his name. Jack Macy.

COLONEL
Three Jacks.

CRUZ
Bring in two ladies and we'll have a full house.

(Silence)

That was your joke, if you'll recall.

COLONEL
You went out looking for people without me?

CRUZ
He came here.

COLONEL
This is today?

CRUZ
Of course. You think I was hiding him somewhere?

COLONEL
I don't know what you have in your lab.

CRUZ
That's right, I forgot to mention I have a dozen people in there. Sorry, but we don't like to invite you to our parties.

(Slight pause, then)

He showed up this morning. If you would've left
half an hour later you would've seen him. Maybe he
would've liked you better than he did me.

COLONEL
How bad was he?

CRUZ
He was very sick. Maybe four, five days since his last
medicine. He came in waving a gun at me, didn't
believe me—

COLONEL
How did he get in?

CRUZ
Excuse me?

COLONEL
You didn't lock the door when I left? He just walked in?

CRUZ
I've been thinking about that lately. Perhaps Stevens
should be a sanctuary. I told Mr. Macy that when he
arrived. He didn't believe me, though, didn't believe me
when I said he could stay here, he could share in our
stash.

COLONEL
I'm impressed you were able to talk him down.

CRUZ

I wasn't. Luckily the sickness made him too weak
to hold a gun while he was coughing. I took the
opportunity I could and subdued him. He's been
sleeping from the half dose I gave him. Wanted to
make certain that his constitution could handle the
power of the medicine.

COLONEL

When do you think we can let him up?

CRUZ

Time will tell. I'm fine, by the way. In case that was
your next question, though I'm doubting it was.

COLONEL

It was a compliment, JC. I assume you can handle
yourself with what you're packing.

CRUZ

Sadly, I was unarmed when Mr. Macy arrived. I
thought it was you, that you had forgotten something,
so I felt no need for protection.

COLONEL

Oh. Well, I'm, I am glad you're okay.

CRUZ

Let's hope that he is able to make a recovery as well.
We are in the touchiest phase of the disease.

COLONEL
Sure. More people is always good. It would've been nice if a woman wandered in, but—

CRUZ
I mean for the future of our species, Colonel.

COLONEL
Do you know something about making babies that I don't?

CRUZ
I'm talking about the disease. The cure I'm trying to—

> *(HE is cut off by MACY making a sound.*
> *It sounds like talking for a second, but*
> *it turns into snoring. HE is out. CRUZ*
> *goes over to MACY and turns his head to*
> *the side and the snoring goes away.)*

COLONEL
Why do you need him for the cure?

CRUZ
I have to try it on someone. And I don't think injecting it into my own veins is the smartest idea.

COLONEL
But if it's a cure, then—

CRUZ
If I get the formula right, it's not as if there's a ding

and balloons fall from the ceiling. I have to test it.

COLONEL
You can try it on me.

CRUZ
All right. I assume you're prepared for how the test
will progress. You're prepared for going off the
medicine for a week to ten days.

COLONEL
I'm sure I could—

CRUZ
You're also, I assume, prepared for the possibility of
me letting you die. Sometimes we only learn what
went wrong through an autopsy.

COLONEL
(Silence, then)
You don't necessarily have to let him die, right?

CRUZ
It depends on how the possible cure progresses. Of
course I don't want to lose a test subject, since we
have so few of them. If it's close though ... we'll cross
that bridge when we come to it, all right?

> *(COLONEL nods and CRUZ goes to his
> lab door and opens it.)*

COLONEL
You can just tell me things, you know? If you can trust me enough to face me without a gun, then you can trust me enough to—

CRUZ
You're right. I'm a solitary person by nature, but ... obviously I don't have that luxury anymore. My apologies, Colonel.

> *(CRUZ exits and COLONEL stares at MACY.*
> *HE thinks for a moment then exits. The*
> *sound of the sistrum. MACY sits up in*
> *bed, still strapped in, but much more*
> *coherent. COLONEL enters with a couple*
> *of cans of fruit. HE grabs a fork and*
> *pulls up a chair next to MACY.)*

COLONEL
You're in luck. I found some pears on a pallet in the back there.

MACY
Good hunting.

COLONEL
Never developed a taste for them. They always seemed like an apple's deformed big brother.

> *(HE opens up the can of pears and*
> *forks one out and feeds it to MACY.*
> *HE'll be feeding him these through*
> *the scene.)*

MACY

I think there's some saying about beggars and choosers. And you're wrong. These are delicious, thanks.

(Slight pause, then)

Medicine tonight?

COLONEL

Tomorrow. You feel like you need it today?

MACY

Well, I feel like I need it all the time, but it's not Slick-based need. It's just regular old junkie need, I reckon. You tried the stuff before all this came down?

COLONEL

Once or twice. You?

MACY

Oh, yeah. I used to work construction. You ever work construction?

COLONEL

No, I never—

MACY

It's good work, decent living, but if you take the wrong step, oh, buddy, that's it for you. And that's what I did, zigged when I should've zagged, and I went ass over teakettle from the second floor to the first without even a staircase between. Broke my leg.

COLONEL
Shit.

> *(His eyes dart to where CRUZ is*
> *working. HE's whipped.)*

MACY
Well, it doesn't feel great. But the good doctor, he
gave me a morphine prescription. Morphine, can you
believe it? I thought that stuff was too dangerous, but
they still use it. Well, they used to. Anyway, doc gives
me way too much, but who am I to say no to a medical
professional? In no time, I've got me the army disease.
You heard of that in the service?

COLONEL
I wasn't actually in—

MACY
Cast comes off, leg feels great, but you know what
feels even better? Popping those pills every day. Boy
did they make everything smooth. Not my life. My life
was a fuck- up. Ruined my marriage, thank God we
didn't have kids to ruin their lives too. And when the
whole world went shithouse, I was fine. For a while.
But my little town didn't have a whole lot of dope, and
it got harder and harder for me to search the outlying
areas. I was pretty messed up in the end, can't really
remember what I did. I know I was following those
signs those. That must've been what got me here.

COLONEL
What signs?

MACY
The goddamn circle and—

COLONEL
You should watch that.

MACY
Watch what?

COLONEL
He doesn't like swearing.

MACY
Is that why I'm still in these straps? If it takes a clean mouth to get me free, then I'll be a choir boy.

COLONEL
Cruz just wants to make sure you're not dangerous.

MACY
Can't you vouch for me?

COLONEL
I'm—

MACY
Or can't you just take them off yourself?

(Silence)

Maybe tomorrow, then.

COLONEL

What sign did you see?

MACY

It's a half-circle with two different sized legs.

> *(HE tries, futilely, to make it in*
> *the air with his finger.)*

COLONEL

Hold on.

> *(COLONEL grabs a folder and a pen*
> *and brings it back. HE draws what*
> *MACY described.)*

Like this?

MACY

Now close off the circle.

> *(COLONEL does.)*

MACY

That's your guy. I saw it on a bunch of signs getting closer and then on the highway exit announcing this place. Took those signs as a sign. Glad I did.

COLONEL

> *(To himself)*

Weird.

MACY

Ol' Cruz there, he's working on the virus?

COLONEL

He's trying to find a cure.

MACY

And you're working for him?

COLONEL

He needs supplies from time to time and we thought it would be better for him to stay in the lab and—

MACY

And for you to do the grunt work.

COLONEL

It's probably for the best.

MACY

You do what you can to survive. But remember that just 'cause that man's got a fancy accent and a lot of smarts, that doesn't give him the right to buffalo you.

COLONEL

He's not doing that. We, we have an understanding.

MACY

You're right. Don't let me stick my nose in it. You do what you need to do. But if you wouldn't mind putting in a good word for me about these

(Showing the restraints)
I'd appreciate it.

COLONEL
I'll do what I can.

MACY
Couldn't ask for anything more.

COLONEL
Last pear in the can.

MACY
Why don't you have it? Maybe you've acquired a taste for them since last time.

> *(COLONEL shrugs and eats the pear piece.*
> *HE grimaces.)*

I guess some things don't change.

(The sound of the sistrum. MACY gets
up from the bed and HE and COLONEL go
to the table. CRUZ comes out with a
few plates and THEY all resume eating
dinner. A few silent bites, then)

MACY
You sure this is canned food? You make it taste fresh, Jack.

CRUZ
Spices. That's the key. Men used to fight wars over

them, travel thousands of miles by ship, just so
their food could taste slightly better. There must be
something to that.

MACY
Well, I'd say it's worth it. My wife, Emily, God rest
her, she was afraid of even putting salt on anything.
She'd watch those news programs where they'd tell
you, "What's in your kitchen cabinet may be killing
you, tune in at six" and she'd say to me, "Jack, I bet
it's salt," and she'd just start dumping it out. Never
bothered to check into the show at six to see if she
were right. I had to start hoarding that stuff like it
was cocaine, keeping it out of Emily's sight and using
it on everything she cooked.

CRUZ
Fascinating.

    (To COLONEL)

How long are your jogs these days?

COLONEL
I can do ten miles easy. Why?

CRUZ
I have an item I need. Material to fix one of the pieces
of equipment that ... it's terribly technical, but the only
place I can imagine it being is in a specialty hardware
store out in the willywags, maybe thirty miles away.

MACY
You could take a car.

CRUZ
The weather has made most cars around here
unusable. Plus the roads are clogged and dangerous.
I would feel better for the Colonel's safety were he to
jog.

COLONEL
Well, I wouldn't jog there, but I could, you know, I'm
sure I could go there in the morning, maybe camp
inside the store for the night, bring it back the next
day. I mean, if that's all right with you.

CRUZ
I'm in no hurry. In fact, I may be able to fix it myself.
I'll let you know if you need to make the trip.

MACY
I could look at it, you know?

CRUZ
Oh, yes?

MACY
I worked in construction. They'd bring me in for arc
welding on occasion, so I've got some experience.

CRUZ
Do you have a lot of experience with electron
microscopes, Mr. Macy?

MACY
Afraid there wasn't much call for that.

CRUZ
Ah, well.

MACY
I would like to help around here, though. Now that you're sure that I'm not dangerous, and, and I'm not blaming you for that. I was dangerous. You were smart to keep me strapped in until you were sure. It's what I would've done. But now that I'm up and around, I could help. I *should* help.

CRUZ
Yes, that's—

MACY
I could go out with the Colonel here, keep him company on his trip, help him carry more shit, stuff, sorry. I'm, uh, I'm grateful to you, Jack, for taking me in when I was such a mess, when the Slick had got my head all crazy. You could've kicked me out, left me to die like a dog in the street, and who would've blamed you? I want to repay that kindness by helping you out, making this place as nice as possible so that you can keep doing the damned important work you're doing.

CRUZ *(Too long of a pause, then)*
Thank you, Mr. Macy.

MACY
> *(Getting up)*

If you'll excuse me, just have to use the facilities.
Spices sure can get your stomach going.

> *(HE exits.)*

CRUZ I owe you an apology, Colonel.

COLONEL
I'm not sure what—

CRUZ
Having to sit and listen to him every day while I'm in
a soundproof room. Does he always go on like that?

COLONEL
Jack's chatty but he's not, he's a good guy. We get
along.

CRUZ
I couldn't stand it, to hear all that yammering in my
ear all the time.

COLONEL
It's good that he's out here and you're in there, then.

CRUZ
Were you this agreeable of a chap when you were a
junkie, Colonel?

COLONEL
I guess. I don't really think I gave it a thought.

CRUZ
I've always seen drug addicts portrayed as wholly selfish, unrepentant, unwilling to move down a trail unless a pile of narcotics sat at the end of said trail.

COLONEL
Yeah, I was like that too. You go to jail, though, get thrown in with a bunch of guys who want the same thing and
can't get it, who you really are comes back out. Situations like that, I'd rather be peaceful and left alone

CRUZ
"Go along to get along." That's what my mother would say. Or maybe she still says it. Maybe she found her own stash of opiates and is living a fulfilled existence on the other side of the Pacific.

COLONEL My mom used to say that too.

CRUZ
And you subscribed to it, I see.

COLONEL
If people leave me alone, don't bother me or mine, then I figure it's just easier to keep my mouth shut.

CRUZ
I never liked that. I never was interested in going *along*. I'd rather not have someone decide where we were going. I prefer to blaze my own trail.

COLONEL
That doesn't surprise me, J.C.

CRUZ
It's served me well, don't you think? God's chosen man, tasked with saving the few that the Almighty hasn't seen fit to wipe out with a flick of his wrist.

COLONEL
And I'm glad to be holed up in here with God's number one guy.
(CRUZ finishes his meal and gets up
from the table.)

CRUZ
Cure's been fashioned, by the way.

COLONEL
Excuse me?

CRUZ The cure for the Slick. I've come up with it. I think.

COLONEL
You're being serious now?

CRUZ

One can never be certain until one tries it out on a test subject, but I have high hopes. Under the microscope I can see the virus being destroyed by the proteins I've synthesized.

COLONEL

This is amazing news. Why aren't we celebrating?

CRUZ A celebration would be premature. Let me finish it up and then we'll test it.

> *(Exiting to the lab)*

Keep your fingers crossed, Colonel.

> *(COLONEL is elated. HE gets up with*
> *his plate and finishes his last bite*
> *with a big smile on his face. The*
> *sound of the sistrum. CRUZ enters*
> *and sits on the floor, head in his*
> *hands. COLONEL enters, wearing a*
> *backpack.)*

COLONEL

You think when you cure the world, the celebration can include a marathon? Because, I've got a feeling I could win. Not a lot of competition but—

> *(HE is cut off by CRUZ keening,*
> *almost howling.)*

J.C., you okay?

CRUZ
Nooo.

COLONEL
            (Looking around)
Was it Macy? Did he go off the deep end or—

CRUZ
Mr. Macy. He's ... oh, Colonel ... it just isn't fair, isn't
fair.

            (HE collapses into tears.)

COLONEL
What's wrong?

            (No answer)

What happened to Jack?

CRUZ
He *died*, Colonel!

COLONEL
He's dead?? Wait, how?

CRUZ
He was—

COLONEL
'cause he was fine when I left yesterday. I get back
today and— this is fuckin' crazy!

CRUZ

Do you want me to tell you or do you want to just curse at me?!?

> *(COLONEL stares at CRUZ for a second.*
> *Is this an act? Finally, HE gives*
> *him a "go ahead" sign.)*

I was mistaken. The cure doesn't work.

COLONEL

You gave him the cure and he up and died? Do you have two bottles that say "cure" and "poison" and you mixed them up?

CRUZ

He didn't "up and die." I gave him the cure four days ago.

COLONEL

No you didn't. We all took—

CRUZ

You took the medicine, Colonel, and while you were indisposed, Mr. Macy and I talked and he chose to take the cure instead.

COLONEL

He didn't say anything to me.

CRUZ

I asked him not to.

COLONEL
Why would you do that?

CRUZ
Because I didn't want there to be an observer bias
in you, always looking for changes in his demeanor,
his appearance, good or bad. If you didn't notice any
difference in him, if the cure mirrored the response to
the medicine, then it was working.

COLONEL
Except it wasn't if he's dead.

CRUZ
It's just not fair. It just isn't.

COLONEL
What went wrong?

CRUZ
Are you a virologist? Because my explanation would
be—

COLONEL
I don't think I'm too dumb to understand how
somebody died.

CRUZ
            (An exhale, then)
He seemed to be fine, and then last night he started
screaming for me. For anybody really, for me, for you,
for his dead wife, his dead child.

COLONEL
Oh yeah?

CRUZ
(Standing to explain)
As best as I can surmise, what I created only delays
the onset of the disease. The cycle is six days not four,
which would be an improvement, but when the virus
comes back, it's two or three times more powerful. The
dormancy phase lets it build up strength. I gave Mr.
Macy some medicine, but it was too late. His body was
far too weak and he ...
(HE dissolves into crocodile tears.)

COLONEL
He kicked the bucket.

CRUZ
I would've thought you would have a bit more
sympathy, all the death we've seen.

COLONEL
Yeah, well ...
(HE shrugs.)
Why'd you send me out, Cruz?

CRUZ
To pick up the parts for the microscope.

COLONEL
I'm asking, why'd you send me out for two days when

things were so touch and go here. Wouldn't it be better
to have an extra pair of hands for a time like that?

CRUZ
What would you have done for Mr. Macy that I couldn't
have done, Colonel?

COLONEL
And shouldn't you have a working microscope *before*
you give out the cure? You know, just to make sure that
what you're giving out will actually work.

CRUZ
I'm already blaming myself so if it makes you feel
better to pile on, then do so, but you seem to be
implying something other than incompetence.

COLONEL
Can I see him?

CRUZ
You want to see the body?

COLONEL
I want to see *him*.

CRUZ
He's on a pallet in the shipping bay.

COLONEL
He's not in your lab? You're not going to do an
autopsy?

CRUZ
I know what killed him. I know what I have to do next time.

COLONEL
You don't want to even double check, just to make sure—

CRUZ
If you'd like you can do an autopsy using all of the medical knowledge you've evidently gained from reading the great novels of the western world. But when you're through, I think Mr. Macy merits a proper funeral.

COLONEL
(Stony)
All right. Fine.

CRUZ
We'll go out tomorrow, inter him in the cemetery a few miles away from here. I'll find an appropriate passage from scripture.
    (Slight pause)
I know you're upset, Colonel. I am too. It's a bleak day indeed.
    (HE goes to the lab door.)

COLONEL
I'd like my dope.

CRUZ
We'll be taking our medicine tonight. It's good to stay on schedule.

COLONEL
I'm saying, I'd like to hold onto my stash. The entire half that's mine.

CRUZ
Ah. I see.

COLONEL
Is there a problem with that?

CRUZ
Of course not.

COLONEL
It is mine, isn't it?

CRUZ
The only reason I'm holding it is because you asked me to.

COLONEL
Changed my mind.

CRUZ
May I ask why?

COLONEL
I don't want to tax your mind with so much

responsibility. You should just have to worry about finding a cure, not taking care of a junkie's stash.

CRUZ
It's no trouble.

COLONEL
And it's even less trouble my way.

CRUZ
(Slight pause, then)
Fair enough.

> *(The sound of the sistrum. CRUZ and COLONEL exit and return with a bible and a shovel, respectively.)*

CRUZ
I think that was a fine service, if I do say so myself.

COLONEL
Yeah?

CRUZ
I'm only a follower not a minister of the Lord, but I think Mr. Macy got a fine farewell. Better than most of the people taken by this wretched plague.

COLONEL
If you say so, Cruz.

> *(COLONEL puts the shovel away.)*

CRUZ
>   *(With false joviality)*

Did you enjoy the Poe?

COLONEL
What are you asking me?

CRUZ
I, the next books on the reading list were works by—

COLONEL
Edgar Allan Poe, right.

CRUZ
Yes.

COLONEL
I like him a lot.

CRUZ
Good to hear. He invented the detective story, you know. "Murders in the Rue Morgue."

COLONEL
That's not a detective story.

CRUZ
I think several literary professors would disagree with you.

COLONEL
There's not a lot of them above ground, so ...

CRUZ
You don't think it's a detective story?

COLONEL
There's a detective in it, but it's a story where when you find out who did it, nobody can be blamed. Not the monkey and not the monkey's owner.

CRUZ
Ape, I believe. Ape, not monkey.

COLONEL
Either way, nobody's really at fault, nobody can be brought to justice, so what's the point of having a detective at all?

CRUZ
Mysteries are made to be solved, aren't they?

COLONEL
If they're puzzles, sure. If it's a crime, though, somebody should be punished.

CRUZ
I've never thought of it that way. I tell you, I am famished. I'm going to get some lunch together. Are you interested?

COLONEL
Not right now.

CRUZ
Suit yourself.

> *(CRUZ goes about getting himself his food. COLONEL thinks of something and pulls the folder out from under his bed.)*

COLONEL
Let me ask you something, Cruz: you recognize this?

CRUZ
It's Egyptian. The Amenta.

COLONEL
What does it mean?

CRUZ
The west bank of the Nile.

COLONEL
That's it?

CRUZ
Far as I know. Why?

COLONEL
Macy said it was on a bunch of signs leading here. I think I've seen one or two of them, but I just thought it was graffiti. Like Space Invaders shit.

CRUZ
The language please.

COLONEL
(Not meaning it)
I'll work on it.

CRUZ
It may mean something else to long-gone gang
members, but it's just the Amenta to me.

COLONEL
Weird.

CRUZ
In a few generations, think of how foreign the golden
arches will seem.

COLONEL
I'm pretty sure the letter M will survive.

CRUZ
Right.

COLONEL
        (A pause, then)
He was calling out for his family?

CRUZ
Mr. Macy?

COLONEL
Yeah.

CRUZ
For his wife.

COLONEL
And his child?

CRUZ
What's this?

COLONEL
That's what you said yesterday.

CRUZ
I don't believe so.

COLONEL
Pretty sure you did.

CRUZ
As far as I know, Mr. Macy had no children. We were both upset, I ... of such things misunderstandings are often made.

COLONEL
            (Slight pause, then)
Sure.

            (The sound of the sistrum. THEY
            both sit at the table, eating in

*silence. COLONEL is looking down
at his can of food, never looking
at CRUZ. CRUZ is slowly eating pasta,
staring at COLONEL. It goes on
this way for thirty seconds, just
tension building. CRUZ is getting
more and more annoyed. COLONEL is
focussing on not looking at CRUZ,
not giving him anything. CRUZ
finishes his bottle of water. HE
gets up.)*

CRUZ
Would you like one?

COLONEL
(Slight pause, then looking up)
What?

CRUZ
I'm getting another bottle of water, Colonel. Would you
like me to get you one?

COLONEL
Sure.

CRUZ
All right.
(HE goes to the exit, and stops.)
If you're not thirsty, I can—

COLONEL
Hey, Cruz? If you feel like getting me a water, I'll drink
it. If you don't, I'll get one myself.

CRUZ
We should talk, Colonel.

COLONEL
Isn't that what we're doing?

CRUZ
About the future.

COLONEL
We should talk about the future?

CRUZ
I think it would be a good idea.

COLONEL
If you say so.

> (CRUZ exits. Quick as a flash,
> COLONEL gets a packet from his
> pocket and empties a powder into
> Cruz's dish of pasta. HE pours
> a bit of water from his bottle
> into the pasta and stirs it up
> with Cruz's spoon. CRUZ enters
> with two bottles of water. Has
> HE noticed something wrong? HE
> drinks from one bottle and puts

the other in front of COLONEL.
HE sits back down at the table.)

CRUZ
So now then.

(But before HE can continue, BOOM
a crazy-loud car crash against the
building. THEY look at each other
then dash outside. The sound of
the sistrum. CRUZ and COLONEL enter
carrying a woman, GWEN on a makeshift
splint of a couple of two by fours, a
sheet, and some duct tape. SHE has a
tourniquet on her hip. Her left leg is
clearly broken and THEY are being
careful about it. GWEN is passed out.
THEY bring her to one of the empty cots.
CRUZ is about to set her down.)

COLONEL
Maybe not the one where Jack was.

CRUZ
I think getting her treatment is more important than
arguing—

COLONEL
We could've put her down on the other bed by now.

CRUZ
Fine.

*(THEY put her down on the cot next to
Colonel's bed.)*

CRUZ
This is me going along to get along.

COLONEL
Appreciate it.

CRUZ
She needs medicine.

COLONEL
She needs a doctor who knows how to set a leg.

CRUZ
I know how to set a leg, Colonel.

COLONEL
Aren't you handy?

CRUZ
She needs medicine to fight off the germ. That's
probably what caused her to crash the car.

COLONEL
I'll take care of it.

CRUZ
I'm happy to do it. I have more than enough medicine.

COLONEL
You go back to finding a cure. I can handle this.

CRUZ
Before I head back to my research, I'll help you put her in restraints.

COLONEL
I don't think she needs them.

CRUZ
Well, I do. Better safe than sorry.

> *(HE removes the restraints from Macy's*
> *cot and goes to put them on Gwen's cot.*
> *COLONEL puts his hand on CRUZ's wrist.)*

COLONEL
Hold on.

CRUZ
You'd be wise to remove your hand, Colonel.

COLONEL
I just don't think she's any threat who needs to—

CRUZ
Colonel?

> *(CRUZ looks ready to destroy COLONEL.*
> *COLONEL removes his hand.)*

You're right, she's probably not any threat. And if she's

in restraints, I guarantee she's not any threat. I prefer
a guarantee to a probably.

COLONEL
Doing this will scare her and she won't trust—

CRUZ
If we don't do this, then you feel free to set her
leg. Make sure you get it right, or it's gangrene and
amputation and death for your new bunkmate. Or you
could do the simple thing I asked and maybe she'll
walk again.

> *(COLONEL stares for a few seconds then
> steps away. CRUZ applies the restraints.)*

Let me know when she wakes up.

> *(HE goes back to the lab. COLONEL sits
> down on his cot next to GWEN. The sound
> of the sistrum. COLONEL has fallen asleep
> and GWEN has woken up. SHE tries to get
> up and realizes SHE's restrained. SHE
> tries looking around, but can't see much,
> just COLONEL next to her.)*

GWEN
> *(Yelling)*

Hey! *Hey!!*

> *(COLONEL wakes up. HE quickly gets
> himself together, making sure CRUZ is
> not out there.)*

COLONEL
Good, you're awake. My name's Jack. You're—

GWEN
Why'm I tied down?

COLONEL
It's for your safety, Miss, please understand.
> *(CRUZ enters silently, observing this.)*

GWEN
Not really sure how tying me down keeps me safe.

COLONEL
It's a little complicated.

GWEN
Why don't you explain it to me while you untie me.

COLONEL
> *(Standing up)*
I just have to make sure that—

GWEN
Untie me or stay away.

COLONEL
This isn't what it looks like. You're safe, I—

GWEN
You're safe. I'm tied up.

> *(COLONEL doesn't move. CRUZ crosses
> to GWEN and unties her.)*

CRUZ
Let me get that for you.

> *(HE goes to her bedside and takes
> off the restraints.*

GWEN
Thank you.

> *(SHE massages her wrists.)*

CRUZ
I must apologize, my dear. The Colonel here feels the need to take certain precautions with our guests. He feels it's necessary for his protection.

GWEN
> *(Not meaning it)*
That's okay.

CRUZ
My name is Jack Cruz.

> *(HE extends his hand. SHE looks at it.)*

GWEN
Gwen Landers.

CRUZ
A pretty name for a pretty lady. Pleased to make your acquaintance, Miss Landers.

GWEN
> *(Not buying it)*

Thank you.

CRUZ

This is my home, Miss Landers. Welcome.

> *(Silence)*

Is there anything I or my associate might fetch you?

GWEN

My things, from my car. It's a black Toyota.

CRUZ

Oh, we know your car. It is, I believe, the one that is wrapped around the far corner of our warehouse. Colonel?

COLONEL

No, I don't need anything. You can just get her stuff, J.C.

CRUZ
> *(His smile disappearing)*

Right.

> *(To GWEN)*

Pardon me.

> *(HE exits.)*

COLONEL

I should explain. We're not so—

GWEN
If you touch me—

COLONEL
I won't.

GWEN
If you touch me, I'll bite off anything near me. It may be your ear, your nose, your dick, I don't care. If you come too close, I'll just start biting. You got it?

COLONEL
Loud and clear.

GWEN
(*An exhale, then*)
You're both named Jack?

COLONEL
You can call me Colonel.

GWEN
Are you military?

COLONEL
Just a nickname.

GWEN
Then I'll stick with Jack. You two have drugs, I guess. Shit, if you're still alive, you must.

COLONEL
We do, but—

GWEN
You're not willing to share? That's fucking ridic—

COLONEL
You shouldn't curse. Not around Cruz. He doesn't like it.

GWEN
End of the world and he has a morals clause going on?

COLONEL
Those are his rules. It'd be smart to obey them.

GWEN
What, are you scared of him?
            (Off of his shrug)
I thought you two were working together.

COLONEL
Marriage of convenience.

GWEN
Sure, good cop bad cop in your fucking rape
warehouse.

COLONEL
Seriously, I wouldn't curse if I were you.
            (Slight pause, then)

GWEN
Is my car working?

COLONEL
Not really. And neither is your leg.

GWEN
Great. Just ... great.

COLONEL
I know how you feel.

GWEN
Did you break your leg too?

COLONEL
No, I ... when I came here I didn't know what I was getting into either.

GWEN
And look how well it's worked out for you.

> *(CRUZ enters with Gwen's bags.)*

CRUZ
I retrieved the lady's things.

COLONEL
Thanks, Mr. Cruz.

CRUZ
Certainly.

(Slight pause)

I, uh, I have a delicate matter to discuss, madam.

GWEN
Need to open up a ladies room now that I'm here?

CRUZ
Your leg. I feel we should set it before it becomes too difficult to do so.

COLONEL
What'll that involve?

CRUZ
Excruciating pain for you, Ms. Landers, I'm afraid. But it will prevent further pain in the future, I can guarantee that.

COLONEL
You wanna do that now? She just got here.

CRUZ
No time like the present.

COLONEL
I don't think she—

GWEN
Just do it.

COLONEL
Yeah?

GWEN
I can handle the pain. You'll watch out for me, help me out as I get better?

CRUZ
We shall both play nursemaid for whatever you need.

GWEN
(To COLONEL)
Jack?

COLONEL
One hundred percent.

GWEN
Then let's do it.

> *(CRUZ motions for COLONEL to brace GWEN and HE takes a hold of her left leg.)*

CRUZ
On three. One, two—

> *(And with a sickening crunch HE sets her leg. SHE screams in agony and passes out from the pain.)*

CRUZ
Good work, Colonel.

COLONEL
Thanks for doing that.

CRUZ
Of course. It's good to have new company, don't you think?

COLONEL
Yeah.

CRUZ
All the more reason to keep working on the cure.

COLONEL
I guess.

CRUZ
I'm sure she'll be happy to hear that we're very close.

COLONEL
Are you very close?

CRUZ
Any day now. I look forward to testing it out.

(CRUZ walks towards his lab.)

COLONEL
Did you still want to talk?

CRUZ
Did I ... what now?

COLONEL
You said you wanted to talk about the future. Before
the crash, you said—

CRUZ
I think the future just crashed into Stevens, don't you?

COLONEL
If you want to try out that cure, I'll take it.

CRUZ
Since I'm the one making the cure, I think that's my
decision.

> *(HE looks over at GWEN.)*

She looks like a sweet person.

> *(HE picks up his dish and drops it into*
> *the sink. HE exits to his lab. COLONEL*
> *curses under his breath. The sound of the*
> *sistrum. Lights down. End of Act I.)*

Act II

Lights up on the warehouse. GWEN is on her cot,
reading. CRUZ is making eggs at the hot plate.
COLONEL enters, carrying oatmeal and water. HE puts
the oatmeal and water together into a pot. HE watches
CRUZ, who is taking his sweet time making his eggs.
CRUZ goes to flip his eggs onto his plate, but instead
flips them over. COLONEL sighs quietly, annoyed.

CRUZ
Problem, Colonel?

COLONEL
Just wondering when you're gonna be done with the
hot plate.

CRUZ
Did you need to use it?

COLONEL
When you're finished.

CRUZ
Does your nurse always make you breakfast, Ms. Landers?

GWEN
When I say please.

CRUZ
You must say please a lot.

COLONEL
So are you done or what?

CRUZ
No. I'm making extra eggs for breakfast. I'm happy to make some more for you two if you like. Nurse to the nurse.

COLONEL
Just let me know when you're finished with it.

CRUZ
You can always go and get another one.

COLONEL
We have another hot plate here?

CRUZ
No, I'm saying you can go *out* and get another one. I'm sure there are a good deal of department stores not ninety minutes walk from here where you could have your pick of hot plates, camping stoves, or grills.

COLONEL
Probably.

CRUZ

Definitely. I've seen them. With the three of us here, I think we could use some extra equipment. Would you mind getting us some?

COLONEL

Maybe next week.

CRUZ

I was under the impression that the things I needed to find the cure you'd get for me.

COLONEL

Really? I was under the impression that a cure was supposed to make you better not dead.

CRUZ

(Slight pause, then)
So no more errands?

COLONEL

When Gwen is up and around, then we'll think about it.

CRUZ

Oh, *we* will? I look forward to that day. As I look forward to my new hot plate.

COLONEL

If you need one so bad, why don't you go out and get it yourself?

CRUZ
This one suits me just fine. I'm patient. God tells us
that patience is a virtue.

> *(THEY stare at each other for a bit.)*

Maybe I'll save my eggs for later. Enjoy your cereal.

> *(HE exits to his lab. COLONEL watches*
> *him go and then puts down the oatmeal.*
> *HE grabs a box of cereal and takes it*
> *back to GWEN. HE sits on the cot*
> *next to her and offers her the open*
> *box. SHE puts her hand in and comes*
> *out with some cereal, which SHE eats.*
> *COLONEL does the same.)*

GWEN
This oatmeal is delicious.

COLONEL
It's my speciality.

GWEN
He sure knows how to ruin a room, doesn't he?

COLONEL
He doesn't help them, that's for sure.

> *(THEY eat cereal as THEY talk.)*

GWEN
Creepy Jesus.

COLONEL
Is that what you call him?

GWEN
Not to his face.

COLONEL
That's a smart move. He's a religious dude, if you haven't noticed.

GWEN
I noticed he talks like he is.

COLONEL
Praying before meals and all that. I figure God lost sight of us a little while ago.

GWEN
Around about when the Whistling Disease popped up.

COLONEL
Yeah. You think every place had a different nickname for The Slick?

GWEN
Let me get on the internet and look it up. Oh, wait.

(COLONEL smiles and gets up.)

COLONEL
All right, let me actually cook that oatmeal.

GWEN
Hold on.

> *(SHE takes his arm and stops him*
> *from leaving.*

COLONEL
What's up? Leg problems?

GWEN
No more than usual. Tell me about him.

COLONEL
I have.

GWEN
You told me how you two met and you told me what
he's working on.

COLONEL
Well, we haven't gotten into our hopes and dreams
quite yet. I haven't been here forever.

GWEN
What if *I* wanted a new hot plate?

COLONEL
There's no need for—

GWEN
Or a pair of scissors to trim up that shaggy mane
of yours. Or a Hostess Sno Ball, still in its wrapper.

Twinkees are the cliche, but I prefer Sno Balls.

COLONEL
Who doesn't like choking on coconut?

GWEN
What if I wanted something we didn't have here?

COLONEL
When you're feeling better, we can go get some together.

GWEN
What if I want those things now? Today.

COLONEL
Do you want them today?

GWEN
No.

COLONEL
Good.

GWEN
What I want today is for you to tell me about him. The real story. And why you won't leave me alone with him.

COLONEL
(An inhale and an exhale, then)
Do you need to know really? Isn't it enough that I won't?

GWEN
I wanna know what to prepare for in case something happens to you.

COLONEL
Nothing's gonna happen to me.

GWEN
Better safe than sorry, right?

COLONEL
What happens if you're both?

>   *(Silence, then)*

I'm afraid of him. Cruz.

GWEN
He threatened you?

COLONEL
No. He threatens me by threatening you.

GWEN
What did he say about me?

COLONEL
Nothing, but—

GWEN
Isn't there the chance that you're just ... that you two have been here together too long? That you're the two guys on the island in the cartoon who start seeing

each other as a hamburger and a hot dog?

COLONEL
I wouldn't eat him without a snakebite kit.

GWEN
(Pressing)
What did he do?

COLONEL
(Slight pause, then)
He's a killer.

GWEN
You have proof of that?

COLONEL
The guy who was in that empty bed, Macy? Cruz killed
him.

GWEN
You saw him do it.

COLONEL
No. No, he sent me out to get stuff, had to stay
overnight, and when I came back the sweet old guy
was dead.

GWEN
But Creepy Jesus didn't confess.

COLONEL
He said he was giving the cure he was working on to Macy and the old guy had a bad reaction to it.

GWEN
That couldn't be true?

COLONEL
It could be. That's the, that's what's fucking with me.

> *(HE unconsciously winces and darts his eyes for a second.)*

GWEN
You're terrified of him.

COLONEL
You know he doesn't like cursing.

GWEN
Well, fuck him. You and I are a majority now, right?

COLONEL
Yeah, but only one of us can walk.

GWEN
For now. Why do you think he killed this Macy guy?

COLONEL
I don't know. Maybe I'm wrong. Maybe he's icy to me because … because, well, I wouldn't be all that warm to somebody who thought I was a murderer either.

GWEN
Great, now he's in your head.

COLONEL
Yeah. Or maybe ... maybe he's just a fucking psycho.

GWEN
Wanna find out and see? Get me my bag.

> *(The sound of the sistrum. GWEN goes*
> *back to sleep. COLONEL takes a bag*
> *of chips and sits at the table. CRUZ*
> *enters and gets a bottle of soda. HE*
> *opens it and takes a swig. HE notices*
> *COLONEL by himself then sees GWEN.)*

CRUZ
You're not eating with your friend?

COLONEL
The lady needed to fix tonight.

CRUZ
Is she not on our schedule? It's two days until—

COLONEL
She'll fix with— Sorry, I know you don't like being
interrupted.

> *(Off of CRUZ waving him off)*

She'll fix with us day after tomorrow too.

CRUZ
She's eating up your supply, Colonel.

COLONEL
Well, that's what happens when junkies get together.

CRUZ
Ms. Landers was already taking the medicine when the sickness hit then.

COLONEL
(Nodding)
Guess what got her started.

CRUZ
She had not found the light of our Lord.

COLONEL
Maybe. But specifically: a car accident.

CRUZ
(A little laugh)
That seems to be her modus operandi.

COLONEL
(Matching him)
Even in the apocalypse, women drivers, huh?

CRUZ
Well, she seems to have taken a shine to you. I'm fine with solitary work in the lab, but I imagine having

companionship must please you.

COLONEL
It does, but you hit on the issue. My dope stash is getting low. I need to restock. You think you could do me a favor, Cruz?

CRUZ
I'm afraid that I've only budgeted so much for myself and research. Any change in that could prove damaging to future prospects for a cure.

COLONEL
No, I'm not asking for any of your stuff. I need to go out and find some, but she gets a little dehydrated after fixing. Would you mind leaving the door to your lab open and if she calls out for me, maybe you bring her some water? That wouldn't be too much trouble, right?

CRUZ
I think I can handle that.

COLONEL
And I'll give you half of what I find. As a thank you. And as an apology for how I've been acting lately. It's, um, it's been a tough few weeks.

CRUZ
For all of us, Colonel.

(*COLONEL rolls up the bag and puts a*

chip clip on it. HE stretches and
tightens up his shoelaces.)

COLONEL
Anything else you need while I'm out?

CRUZ
You really like her, don't you?

COLONEL
I have a little crush on her, sure. If circumstances were different ...

CRUZ
They might be soon enough. A cure could be right around the corner.

COLONEL
Fingers crossed.

CRUZ
Colonel, I understand that knowing I'm a man of faith, you might be reluctant to ... progress any further with Ms. Landers, physically. But we are a society with a dearth of ministers and marriage licenses, so if you both agree to something, don't let me stand in the way of passion.

COLONEL
(Forcing a smile)
I appreciate that.

(Awkward pause)

So we're good?

CRUZ

Go and bring back medicine for you and your lady.
We'll be fine here at Stevens.

COLONEL

Thanks, J.C.

>   *(HE grabs a duffel bag and jogs out*
>   *with it. CRUZ watches him go and*
>   *then stares at GWEN. HE takes a swig*
>   *and then goes to GWEN.)*

CRUZ

Ms. Landers, I wanted to let you know that your
paramour is off to procure some medicine for the two
of you. He is concerned that you're taking too much of
it, but I'm sure he'll never voice those concerns to you.
We take it to ward off the sickness, not to touch the
face of a false god.

GWEN

>   *(Quietly)*

Pizz bangmuh wawazza.

CRUZ

I'm afraid I don't speak junkie.

GWEN
> *(A little louder)*

Wazza.

CRUZ

Ah. Why didn't you say so?

> *(HE goes and grabs a bottle of water.*
> *HE opens and puts it next to her,*
> *just out of arm's reach. SHE lolls*
> *her head towards it and tries to*
> *lift up her left arm but it's no*
> *good. Her right arm stays underneath*
> *the covers. CRUZ just watches her.)*

GWEN

Pizz. Da wazza.

CRUZ

You can't get it yourself? That's unfortunate.

> *(HE sits down on an empty cot next*
> *to her.)*

You want me to pour it into your mouth? That could prove dangerous. You might drown and the Colonel will think that I've done something to you. To punish him, as if he's the only person who matters in the world. Let me help out.

> *(HE lifts her up a little so that SHE is*
> *upright and HE gives her a drink of water.*
> *His actions are careful, almost tender.*
> *HE lowers her back down gently.)*

GWEN
Thanzz.

CRUZ
Of course, Ms. Landers. I'm your friend too. You rest up now.

> *(HE leaves her and exits to his lab.*
> *SHE relaxes a bit, her eyes moving*
> *more deliberately. CRUZ comes back*
> *out, moving with some speed, holding*
> *a pair of tongs. HE sits next to*
> *her again, surprising her.)*

If you two think I'm so stupid then why would you be scared of me?

GWEN
Wuzz yuu tozzin—?

CRUZ
> *(Mimicking her)*

Wuzz yuu tozzin abaah? I'ze so stoned I canzent see straight.

> *(Back to normal)*

Keep pretending if you like. This is to what? To prove to the Colonel that I'm the scary monster he thinks I am? I'm trying to find a cure for you people and this is how I'm treated? Disgusting.

GWEN
I juzz nee sah wazza fah—

CRUZ
What's in your right hand? The one you've got hidden under there?

GWEN
I juzz nee—

CRUZ
One way to find out.

> *(HE takes his tongs and snaps at the*
> *knee of her hurt leg. SHE yells out*
> *in pain and both hands instinctively*
> *go for her knee. SHE drops something*
> *on the cot. CRUZ, quick as can be,*
> *reaches under the covers and comes out*
> *with a taser. HE admires it.)*

Taser, very nice. And I assume the Colonel will be back here in about thirty seconds after hearing you scream. I mean, he never really left, correct?

> *(HE tosses the taser back to her.*
> *HE walks to his lab door. COLONEL*
> *enters in a hurry, but stops when*
> *HE sees GWEN is fine and that CRUZ*
> *isn't near her.)*

Great plan, guys.

> *(HE exits to the lab. COLONEL looks*
> *to GWEN, who is still nursing her*
> *leg. SHE gives him an "I'm sorry" look.*
> *The sound of the sistrum. Very dim*
> *lighting in the warehouse. GWEN and*

*COLONEL are asleep in cots that have
been pulled up close to each other.
CRUZ is standing behind them. His
left hand is in his pocket and HE
begins breathing a bit heavier. GWEN's
eyes open and SHE quickly figures
out what's going on. SHE doesn't
move but looks over to COLONEL. SHE
tries to will him awake with her eyes,
but no luck. CRUZ finishes with an
exhale and a slight grunt. HE exits
to his lab. SHE leans over and puts
her hand on COLONEL to wake him. When
HE opens his eyes, SHE puts a finger
up to her mouth. THEY speak quietly.)*

COLONEL
Are you okay?

GWEN
I'm fine.

COLONEL
What happened?

GWEN
He was here. Behind us.

COLONEL
I didn't mean to fall asleep. I thought I—

GWEN
        (Waving him off)
I'm fine, Colonel.

COLONEL
Did he say anything to you?

GWEN
He was jerking off.

COLONEL
You're serious?

GWEN
Not something I would make up.

COLONEL
No, of course not. Was ... were you exposed or—
        (Off of her glare)
I'm not blaming you, Gwen.

GWEN
The covers were up to my neck. It's fucking freezing in here. I've worn a lot less, I think ... God, it's awful.

COLONEL
What?

GWEN
I think he was getting off on the idea of killing us. I think that's better than porn to him. I think that *is*

porn to him.

COLONEL
(Getting up)
Well, there's no way I'm sleeping now.

GWEN
Yeah, me neither.
(Slight pause)
You know what I miss? Shitty TV.

COLONEL
That's what you miss?

GWEN
I didn't say it was the only thing I missed. I used to
watch those cheap History Channel things all the time
when I couldn't sleep. You know, "How Did Stonehenge
Happen," "Mysteries of the Pyramids," things like that,
where they just talk about a strange thing without
ever solving it. I'd drift off to those so much that
I started recording them so I could use them like
sleeping pills later. I'd love to have them now.

COLONEL
Sure.
(Remembering something)
You know about the pyramids?

GWEN
I'm sure something seeped in. Did you want to rebuild

Khufu, Khafra, and Menkaura?

>   *(A little laugh)*

Wow, I can't believe I retained that.

>   *(COLONEL grabs the folder from under his bed.)*

COLONEL
Do you know this? The Amenta?

GWEN
Sure. The pyramids were giant tombs. They'd use that.

COLONEL
It means death?

GWEN
Land of the dead. The underworld.

COLONEL
Also known as Stevens.

>   *(A slight pause, then)*

We've gotta get out of here.

GWEN
Yeah, but he's not gonna let us go.

COLONEL
Then we stop him. There's no way I'm staying here, waiting for him to kill one of us.

GWEN
He'll kill me not you.

COLONEL
He hates me.

GWEN
That's why he'll kill me. Hey, Colonel?

COLONEL
Yeah?

> *(HE turns to her and SHE takes his face
> in her hands and kisses him. It's a long,
> sweet kiss. THEY break off.)*

GWEN
We'll think of something.

COLONEL
Yeah.

GWEN
He has to sleep sometime.

COLONEL
I hope.

> *(The sound of the sistrum. COLONEL
> returns to the kitchen and stirs
> some oatmeal on the stove. GWEN
> eats oatmeal in her bed. CRUZ
> comes out and doesn't acknowledge*

the two of them. HE gets some
water and head back to the lab.
HE stops at Gwen's voice.)

GWEN
You're not gonna say anything to him?

CRUZ
Excuse me?

GWEN
Not you. *Him.*

COLONEL
What do you want me to say?

GWEN
You could apologize for starters?

COLONEL
I'm not gonna—

GWEN
Three people left in the world and you still have pride?
Ridiculous.

COLONEL
There are more than three—

CRUZ
I have work to do. I have no interest in being involved
in your bickering.

GWEN

Fine, if you won't, then I will. I'm sorry, Jack.

CRUZ

(Not really believing)

You are?

GWEN

He's paranoid. He got my head all full of—

COLONEL

Well, wouldn't you be paranoid? After everything
that's happened in the world, wouldn't you be a little
uneasy?

GWEN

I would check the facts. If I had two good legs I'd do
just that, but ...

(To CRUZ)

Anyway, I'm sorry. Colonel's paranoia sorta seeped
into my head and I treated you badly. I apologize.

COLONEL

(Still a bit unsure)

Thank you, Ms. Landers.

GWEN

Gwen, please.

(Slight pause, then)

So you're not gonna say anything?

COLONEL
J.C. and I have an understanding.

GWEN
That's just dumb man talk for you not wanting to
admit you're wrong. The guy saved your life, Colonel.

CRUZ
I merely gave him a place to stay.

GWEN
And where would he be if you hadn't done that? He'd
be dead in a gutter with a needle in his arm. Just like
I'd be dead in my jeep. So maybe you say you're sorry
and this place can be a lot less tense than it's been.

COLONEL
     (An exhale, then)
I'm sorry, Cruz.

CRUZ
It's not necessary.

COLONEL
No, she's right. I'm just ... I was messed up about Macy.
He was, I don't know, he was hope and when he didn't
make it, I, I should've blamed the Slick, not the guy
trying to stop it. So I really am sorry.

CRUZ
Apology accepted.

COLONEL
And if you, I'm serious, if you need more things for the cure, I'm on it. You just make a list.

CRUZ
I'm glad to hear that.

> *(HE offers his hand and THEY shake on it. CRUZ shows off his strength in that shake.)*

COLONEL
All the muscles in the world, right?

CRUZ

> *(A slight smile)*

Perhaps, Colonel.

> *(HE goes back to the lab.)*

GWEN
Hungry?

CRUZ
Excuse me?

GWEN
Colonel found some cinnamon and we're enjoying some very decadent oatmeal. I was gonna have seconds, but—

CRUZ
I'm content, thanks.

GWEN
Hard-working man like yourself, are you sure?

CRUZ
(Slight pause, then)
If it's no trouble.

GWEN
No trouble at all. Garcon?

COLONEL
No trouble for the bedridden.
(HE ladles up some oatmeal)
Here you are, Cruz.
(HE gives CRUZ the bowl and picks up his own. THEY sit at the table, talking to GWEN. CRUZ digs into his oatmeal, eating quickly.)

GWEN
I think we should get a cat.

COLONEL
Are you serious?

CRUZ
They did survive the Slick.

GWEN
Are either of you allegic?

CRUZ
Allergies are a fiction used as excuses for weak constitutions.

COLONEL
Well, my constitution is super weak when bees are around. Cats are fine, though.

CRUZ
What kind of cat?

GWEN
I don't know. Black maybe.

CRUZ
Not worried about bad luck?

GWEN
I think I can handle it at this point.

(CRUZ picks up a book from the table.)

COLONEL
Yeah, that's mine.

CRUZ
Well, I didn't think Gwen was reading it.

COLONEL
Right.

CRUZ
Dirty book, Colonel.

COLONEL
Oh yeah?

CRUZ
Banned for being ... well, whatever they ban books for being. Too vulgar, too true.

COLONEL
Ah.

CRUZ
Do you find it that? Too vulgar or too true?

COLONEL
I'm not far enough into it to say.

CRUZ
Well, would you mind if I ...?

COLONEL
All yours.

> *(CRUZ starts reading the book.*
> *GWEN drops her spoon.)*

GWEN

Little help here?

COLONEL

I've got it.

> *(HE gets up and goes to GWEN.*
> *HE gets the spoon. HE mouths*
> *"A cat?" SHE shrugs. CRUZ eyes*
> *go heavy for a moment and then*
> *his head dips. HE brings his*
> *head back up. Then it dips again,*
> *(CONT'D)*
> *lower this time. GWEN and COLONEL*
> *stare at him. HE brings his head*
> *back up, but too far, his eyes*
> *up to the ceiling. HE's back to*
> *normal and HE tries to read a*
> *few more words, but his head dips*
> *one more time. Very low this time.*
> *COLONEL and GWEN look to each*
> *other. Is that it? Then CRUZ*
> *gets up quickly and wheels around*
> *and stares at GWEN and COLONEL.*
> *HE knows. GWEN and COLONEL grab hands.)*

CRUZ

(Angrier than anyone has ever been) You ...

> *(GWEN screams. CRUZ falls back in*
> *his seat and his head plops onto*
> *the table. HE drops the book and*
> *COLONEL screams again. GWEN starts*

> *moving in the bed as best as SHE*
> *can, hitting the sheets with her*
> *hands and yelping in terrified*
> *triumph. COLONEL puts his arm*
> *around her to calm her down. SHE*
> *finally stops.)*

COLONEL
It worked. I can't believe it worked. I tried to use that mickey before you got here, but you showed up, not that you ruined it, but there wasn't—

GWEN
Colonel?

COLONEL
Yeah?

GWEN
Chair.

COLONEL
Got it.

> *(HE runs out. GWEN stares at CRUZ,*
> *breathing hard, willing him not to*
> *wake up. HE doesn't move. COLONEL*
> *comes in with a wheelchair. HE*
> *picks up GWEN but doesn't put her*
> *down immediately.)*
> *I want a good position so your leg doesn't—*

GWEN

Fuck my leg. Just get me into the chair.

> *(HE puts her into the wheelchair, with
> a small groan of pain from her. HE
> grabs two duffel bags from under the
> beds and wheels her away from the beds,
> closer to the entrance.)*

COLONEL

We're really doing this, aren't we?

GWEN

We're not there yet. In case he wakes up?

COLONEL

Right.

> *(HE goes to CRUZ's belt and takes
> off the big keyring. COLONEL is
> about to let CRUZ go when HE
> reaches around and opens CRUZ's
> jacket. HE unhooks the holster
> and takes it off of CRUZ.)*

GWEN

You got the gun?

> *(COLONEL shows that the holster is
> empty.)*

COLONEL

Not on him, I'm afraid.

GWEN

It's in the lab then. Go grab it.

COLONEL

I don't think that's a great idea.

GWEN

Well, I can't go get it and we need it. Grab that and grab his drugs. It's the settlement you're getting in this divorce from Jack Cruz.

COLONEL

Fine, but you're coming with me.

> *(HE wheels her over to the lab door. HE*
> *tries to take her into the lab, but*
> *her chair won't fit. HE opens a duffel*
> *bag and pulls out the taser. HE hands*
> *it and the keys to her, and kisses her.)*

COLONEL

Scream if you see anything.

GWEN

Hurry.

> *(HE exits to the lab. GWEN sits there*
> *watching CRUZ, holding the taser, almost*
> *vibrating with tension. After fifteen*
> *seconds of her heavy breathing)*

Colonel?

COLONEL *(OFF)*
I've got the gun.

GWEN
Good. Drugs?

COLONEL *(OFF)*
I don't know where they are. Can't find them anywhere.

GWEN
Just get back—

COLONEL *(OFF)*
And all the science shit is still in the boxes I brought it in. He hasn't done a thing.

> *(CRUZ moves so slightly and GWEN inhales*
> *sharply. SHE is about to scream, but it's*
> *nothing. SHE exhales slowly, making sure.*
> *SHE shakes her head a little at her*
> *nervousness. A small, humorless laugh,*
> *and then SHE turns her head slightly to*
> *the door of the lab.)*

GWEN
Hey, Colonel?

> *(Fast as lightning, CRUZ runs at GWEN.*
> *SHE screams and the lights go out on*
> *the stage. The sound of the door of*
> *the lab slamming and then COLONEL*
> *beating on it. The sound of the*
> *sistrum, longer this time. When it*

*ends it's replaced by a CLICK of a
padlock opening and then dropping to
the floor. Lights up on the warehouse.
The wheelchair is gone. The duffel
bags are gone. Everyone is gone. The
padlock sits on the floor next to the
lab door. It slowly opens, and the
barrel of the gun comes out first.
COLONEL's eye is at the cracked open
door, and, finding nothing, HE opens
the door, holding tightly to the gun
with one hand, a banker's box in the
other, and leans against the door of
the lab, scanning the area.)*

COLONEL
Cruz! CRUZ!!

(Nothing)

You want to kill somebody so bad, you kill me. It was
my idea. You want to torture me until I lose it from the
Slick, you do that. She wasn't a part of it, okay? She
didn't even know it was coming?

(Nothing)

Cruz?

*(A slight noise? A whimper? It's hard
to tell, but there's something)*

You wanna talk? Because if you don't want to take that
offer, I've got another one for you.

*(Nothing. HE goes to the outer door
and tries it. There's now a padlock*

on the other side.)

I found your stash. I mean, I found both stashes. The
drugs you never touched, and the ... the *shit* you use to
really get off. Wallets of dead people, obituaries,

> *(Taking out obits and videotapes and*
> *waving them around, dumping them out)*

fingernail clippings, and ... God, I think there's a
fucking ear in here. I got your best stuff and I'll trade
it for her life. If you don't give me Gwen, I take out
one of the bunsen burners I brought you, the ones you
never use, and I hook it up to that natural gas tank
that's never been tapped, and I burn your fucking lab
to the ground. I burn your entire stash. All the fucked-
up books, the souvenirs, the videotapes of ... I mean,
how long have you been killing, Cruz? Some of them go
back to when you were, shit, twelve or so, right?

> *(That slight noise again. A whimper,*
> *maybe a skittering. HE goes back to*
> *the lab door.)*

Were you furious at the Slick for killing all of the
people you wanted to? Were you mad that it took your
future victims? Well, you give me Gwen or I burn all
your memories. Macy and this Laura who "left" and all
of the people unlucky enough to cross paths with you,
you fuckin' monster. You say you run a fair house, well
I think this is fair. I'll give you five to say something
and then I burn this bag of your stash. Once I do that,
I give you ten minutes and the whole place goes up.
Five, four, three, t—

> *(The lock on the outer door opens.*
> *COLONEL stares, unwilling to move.*
> *HE finally makes his way to there,*
> *takes a breath, and flings open the*
> *outer door with his left hand, right*
> *hand on the gun. There is nobody there.)*

Cruz?

> *(No answer.)*

Cruz.

> *(Still nothing. Louder)*

Answer me, damn you.

> *(A longer silence. Louder still)*

Answer me!

> *(The generator coughs and dies, lights*
> *out, only the display glow of some*
> *battery powered items remains. Panicked)*

Shit.

> *(HE spins around. A figure appears on*
> *the other side of the room. COLONEL*
> *unloads on it, firing until the gun goes click. As HE is*
> *firing,)*

COLONEL

> *(Calmly and quietly)*

Die, die, die, die, die.

> *(When his gun runs out of bullets*
> *there is just a clicking. The*
> *generator kicks back to life and*

the lights come on. There is no
corpse, just a scarecrow with a
broom handle in its back. COLONEL
goes to see it and realizes his
mistake. HE runs back to the
outer door, looking for a clip
in his jeans. HE finds one and
goes to reload, but it's too late
when the real CRUZ appears in the
doorway. HE has a rifle in his
hands and it's pointed at COLONEL.
Lights down. Then the sound of the
rifle being fired, the sound of a
beanbag hitting COLONEL, and then
COLONEL dropping to the floor.
The sound of the sistrum. Lights up
on the warehouse (days?) later.
COLONEL is waking up in his bed.
HE is slow to move. HE lifts his
arms, expecting to find restraints,
but HE is free to move. Has this
all been a dream? HE rolls over
and sees GWEN in bed next to him,
her back to him.)

COLONEL
   (Quietly)
Oh God, Gwen, you wouldn't believe it. I had the
weirdest fucking dream.

   (No response from GWEN.)
Are you all right?

GWEN

> *(In a very strange voice)*

Good morning, honey? How did we sleep?

> *(COLONEL gets up and when HE does,*
> *CRUZ head pops up from the covers*
> *of Gwen's bed. HE did the voice.)*

CRUZ

I gave her back to you like you asked. Do we still have a deal?

> *(HE hops out of bed, no shirt on,*
> *a wet spot on the crotch of his*
> *pants. The lifeless corpse of*
> *GWEN lolls over. COLONEL takes*
> *a half step back from it, a sharp*
> *inhale of air. HE looks up at*
> *CRUZ, who gives him a big smile.)*

Back to the bargaining table, I guess.

> *(CRUZ turns his back to COLONEL*
> *and walks back to the lab. We*
> *can see a giant tattoo of an*
> *Amenta on his back. COLONEL*
> *flexes his fingers, ready to*
> *charge at CRUZ, and then his*
> *shoulders slump. HE watches*
> *COLONEL go and goes back to his*
> *cot. HE takes Gwen's hand and*
> *curls up into the fetal position.*
> *The sound of the sistrum. COLONEL*
> *is now alone in the warehouse.*

*GWEN is gone and there's a tablecloth
on the kitchen table. HE gets up
and goes to the outer door and pulls
on it, but it's locked. The sound of
something moving behind COLONEL.
HE turns around.)*

COLONEL

(Quietly)

Cruz?

*(A puppet pops from under the table
and it speaks with Cruz's version
of Gwen's voice.)*

CRUZ

Good morning, honey? How did we sleep?

*(COLONEL stares at the puppet. HE
takes a step closer and realizes that
it's not a puppet. It's Gwen's
severed head. CRUZ comes out from
under the table, holding the head on
his fist.)*

CRUZ

What's the matter, sweetie? Cat got your tongue?

*(No answer. CRUZ bounces the head
through the air towards COLONEL.
COLONEL backs up until HE hits
the door and can't move. CRUZ
gets the head close to COLONEL's
face)*

CRUZ

No kiss, honey?

> *(COLONEL doesn't move. CRUZ shrugs*
> *and then HE turns it back to*
> *himself and gives it a big kiss.)*

CRUZ

> *(In his normal voice)*

Bad choice.

> *(HE opens up Gwen's mouth and pulls*
> *out a key. HE puts the key in his*
> *pocket and bounces the head out of*
> *the room with him. Back to Gwen's voice.)*

Dooptee-dooptee-doo. Dooptee-doo.

> *(COLONEL slides down the wall and*
> *sits on the floor. HE is shaken.*
> *The sound of the sistrum. COLONEL*
> *has passed out on the floor. CRUZ*
> *comes in, wearing a tank top, and*
> *grabs COLONEL, picking him up and*
> *putting him in a chair.)*

CRUZ

Here now, we can't have you sleeping on the floor.
What would the lady of the house think?

> *(No response)*

Still giving me the silent treatment, eh?

> *(HE goes and gets two bottles of water.*
> *HE puts one in front of COLONEL and*
> *drinks from the other.)*

COLONEL
Why'd you do it?

> *(A smile comes across CRUZ's face.*
> *Finally, a response.)*

CRUZ
You two tried to kill me.

COLONEL
We just wanted to leave. And that's—

CRUZ
You could've just asked. I wasn't holding you here.
That was all in your head. And then you did that to me
and I had to ... well, I had to do *something*, Colonel,
didn't I?

> *(A swig of water.)*

It was the funniest thing. When I cut her throat, she
broke wind. Just a slash and then

> *(Making a breaking wind noise)*

Talk about ruining a moment.

COLONEL
That's not what I'm asking.

CRUZ

> *(Ignoring him)*

I know you're unhappy you didn't get to bed your
young maiden fair, but you didn't miss much. Plus her
snatch needed a good shave.

COLONEL
>*(Suddenly snarling)*

And how many geriatrics did you bed back at the hospice?

CRUZ
>*(A slight pause)*

You saw my papers in there? My history.

COLONEL

I saw that somebody was crazy enough to give you a job working with the dying. They didn't know that was like giving a pedophile a job as a scout troop leader.

CRUZ

It was one of the best jobs I ever had. I miss it on occasions. And you want to know what about my time there? How many—

COLONEL

How many old ladies did you *fuck*?

CRUZ

Oh. Sixteen. Does that answer all your questions?

COLONEL

Why'd you do it?

CRUZ

Have you not been paying attention? You two tried to kill me and—

COLONEL

Asshole, I'm asking: why didn't you kill me?

CRUZ

Ahhh. Why didn't you say so?

> *(HE giggles and takes a swig of water.)*

I'm not telling.

> *(COLONEL makes a move to attack CRUZ,*
> *but CRUZ easily swats him away. HE*
> *puts his hand on COLONEL's neck.)*

Okay, fine, you beat it out of me. I didn't kill you because I can't decide what's a better punishment for you: killing you or letting you live.

> *(HE pats COLONEL on the chest and sits back down.)*

COLONEL

> *(Pointing to Cruz's tattoo)*

Nice tat.

CRUZ

The Amenta? You know nothing of the Amenta.

COLONEL

Land of the dead.

CRUZ

> *(Smiling)*

It came to me in a dream from the Almighty. God awarded me my ensign, and orchestrated my present survival, and all that we see here.

COLONEL
God's doing a real bang-up fuckin' job.

CRUZ
Consider the chances that I would be inspired to adopt
the ancient and prestigious Amenta, the Land of the
Dead, and then become the king of just such a place.

COLONEL
And God put you on dope too? To make you 'king?'

CRUZ
I was only on narcotics for a few months. So I could
learn what you addicts feel. Since then I've been able
to reproduce that feeling without any drugs. That's *my*
cure.

COLONEL
How do you do it?

CRUZ
You find the thing that invigorates you, that makes
your life complete, that lets your brain and body surge
beyond anything you thought possible, and you think
only of that.

COLONEL
For me that *is* what dope was.

CRUZ
For me, it's death. Death is the ultimate will of the
Almighty. It is the exit of this stupid illusion, an

awakening into the grandest of reality, denied us for these seasons of life. Did you have time to see all of my history in there? I helped dozens into this beautiful process as a job, and then I killed openly before the world ended, seeing if I would get caught, but God steered me through. I am His golden boy, the prophet of a new empire, a non-empire, a kingdom without a population. A world fit for Him, the inventor of death.

COLONEL
If you love death so much, why don't you just kill yourself?

CRUZ
Oh, but that would spoil the fun! Why experience one death, when I can revel in hundreds?

> *(An inhale then an exhale. HE is*
> *beaming.)*

I'll kill you, Colonel. At some point. But not today.

> *(HE gets up.)*

You should eat something.

COLONEL
I'm not hungry.

CRUZ
That's not gonna work. I decide your death, not you. So eat something, or I'll bring the head back. And I won't just kiss it this time.

> *(A standoff and then COLONEL grabs a*

> *bag of chips and opens it. HE eats*
> *a few. CRUZ pats him on the back.)*

Good man.

> *(CRUZ goes to his lab. COLONEL's voice stops him.)*

COLONEL
All the stuff you ever had me get, that was just for show? You had no intention on trying to find a cure?

CRUZ
Some of it was for show. No need for test tubes. But you were helping me with a very important project. You'll see about that soon enough.

COLONEL
I bet.

> *(Slight pause, then)*

When do I fix?

CRUZ
What?

COLONEL
It's been more than four days. When do I get more dope?

CRUZ
Who says you do?

> *(HE exits. The sound of the sistrum.*
> *A darkness descends over Stevens. The*
> *sistrum continues, increasing in volume,*

until the lights come back up. The
sound of coughing gets louder and
louder, with a breathing that becomes
more and more labored. Then the
breathing and coughing sputter out
and stop altogether. Then a sound
like a fist hitting a chest and a
gasp for air. Lights back up on
Stevens. CRUZ is in the kitchen eating
eggs with ketchup on them. COLONEL
wakes up in his cot and looks around.
HE is furious at what he sees. HE gets
up and storms into the kitchen, getting
in CRUZ's face.)

COLONEL
What did you do?

CRUZ
Mornin', sunshine.

COLONEL
What the fuck did you do?!?

CRUZ
How are you feeling? You look great.

COLONEL
You let me die.

CRUZ
Yes. I thought you'd be happier. I did what you asked.

COLONEL
You let The Slick take me over, no drugs for like ten days.

CRUZ
Fourteen days. A full two weeks.

COLONEL
Then you let me die from it.

CRUZ
Yes. Which is what you wanted.

COLONEL
So is this hell? Because it sure as fuck isn't heaven.

CRUZ
I let you die. And then I plunged a needle into your arm and brought you back. Isn't life wonderful? Don't you appreciate more now that you got it back? You finally know what you'd be missing.

COLONEL
You could've been a human being for once and just let me go.

CRUZ
Sure. But what fun would that be?

COLONEL
I was free.

CRUZ

Death, the grandest of reality. Now you can experience it every two weeks. Aren't you lucky?

COLONEL
(Slight pause)
That's your plan, huh?

CRUZ

No. That's God's plan.

> *(HE takes one more bite of eggs and then drops the dish in the sink.)*

All right, have to get back at it. Today is the first day of the rest of your two week life, Colonel. Enjoy it!

> *(CRUZ exits to his lab.)*

Welcome back, Colonel. Glad to have you around.

> *(HE exits. COLONEL is in a rage.*
> *HE tears up the room, ripping the*
> *sheets off a cot and flipping it over.*
> *HE kicks the bucket of money over.*
> *HE goes to sweep the table of its items,*
> *and then HE realizes something.*
> *HE takes the ketchup to the sink and*
> *throws the bottle in the sink.*
> *HE picks up a glass shard from the sink*
> *and goes to his cot. HE looks behind him,*
> *making sure that HE is alone.*
> *HE sits there with a shard in one*
> *hand and contemplates his wrist.*
> *HE swallows and then shakes his head.)*

COLONEL
Fuck him.

> *(HE goes to clean up the sink and*
> *picks up a ketchup-covered shard.*
> *HE studies it. HE is forming an*
> *idea. The sound of the sistrum.*
> *Lights up on Stevens, morning. COLONEL*
> *is on his side sleeping in his cot.*
> *CRUZ enters and goes through his*
> *morning rituals, (putting bottled water*
> *on the stove, getting a bowl and some oatmeal ready,*
> *etc.) singing as HE does.)*

CRUZ

> *(Singing)*

A mighty fortress is our God, a bulwark never failing.
Our helper He, amid the flood of mortal ills prevailing:
For still our ancient foe doth seek to work us woe;
His craft and power are great, and, armed with cruel
hate, On earth is not his equal.

> *(Speaking)*

Sing with me, Colonel.

> *(Singing)*

A mighty fortress is our ...

COLONEL

> *(Weakly)*

I'm escaping, Cruz.

CRUZ *(Laughing)*
Not bloody likely.

COLONEL
>   *(As before)*
Shows what you know.

>   *(COLONEL turns over in bed and CRUZ*
>   *sees that COLONEL's left arm and lap*
>   *are streaked with blood. HE is holding*
>   *a bloodied glass shard in his right*
>   *hand. CRUZ runs to him.)*

CRUZ
Colonel!

>   *(HE grabs the glass shard and throws*
>   *it away. HE is breathing hard,*
>   *staring at CRUZ.)*

CRUZ *(Quietly)*
You're not allowed to do that. Not like Laura.

>   *(CRUZ goes to the kitchen and grabs*
>   *some paper towels.)*

COLONEL
That's how she escaped, huh? I'll tell her you say hi.

CRUZ
Save your strength.

COLONEL
Fuck that.

*(CRUZ takes the paper towels and tries to
stanch the bleeding on COLONEL's wrist.)*

CRUZ
I'm not going to let you die. We have too many plans.
The radio's not ready yet.

COLONEL
What radio?

CRUZ
We must bring more people here. I've been
constructing a transmitter in there. "Come to Stevens,"
the message will say to anyone with a ham radio, a
walkie talkie, anything that can receive signals. "Come
to Stevens, we have the cure." I want you to be here to
welcome them with me.

COLONEL
I ... I think you stopped the bleeding.

CRUZ
If you hold them here, I'll find some gauze.

COLONEL
I'm feeling better than before. I read this book about
the Dark Ages, how people would go for a bloodletting
to improve their health. The book called it bunk, but
maybe there's something to it.

CRUZ
Can I trust you to hold the ... you smell odd, Colonel.

COLONEL
Heinz 57, J.C.

CRUZ
I don't understand.

COLONEL
(*Voice back to normal*)

I think those work as last words.

> (*COLONEL reaches into his shirt
> and pulls out another shard and
> stabs CRUZ in the neck with it.
> CRUZ roars in pain and COLONEL
> pushes him off the bed. CRUZ tries
> to chase after COLONEL, but COLONEL
> pushes him away, pushing him down
> to the floor. COLONEL grabs a bag
> from under his bed. HE goes to the
> door. It's locked. CRUZ laughs and
> holds up the keys, but HE is clearly
> getting weaker. COLONEL gets all
> his courage together and HE runs up
> and kicks CRUZ straight in the balls.
> CRUZ starts coughing and HE drops the
> keys. COLONEL picks up the keys. HE
> goes to the door and unlocks it.*)

> (*To CRUZ, and to himself?*)

You're dead, you're dead, you're fucking dead.

> (*HE exits, finally. One last roar of
> pain from CRUZ and then it stops. The*

sound of the sistrum and lights down on
Stevens. Lights up on a abandoned area,
miles away from Stevens. COLONEL is
going through some supplies that were
left there. HE finds some canned food
and he throws it in his duffel bag. HE
tosses away a few other items and keeps
some medication that HE finds. The last
thing HE finds is a walkie-talkie. HE
contemplates throwing it away, but then
HE turns it on. There's still juice left
in it. Static, static. COLONEL presses
the button to talk.)

COLONEL
Hello, hello? Anybody out there? Hello?

(Static, static. HE changes the frequency
and presses the button again.)

Hello? Anybody?

(Static, static. HE changes the frequency
and presses the button, but the second
before HE does, there's a blurt of sound
from the walkie-talkie. HE lets his
finger off the button and there's a beep,
followed by a familiar voice.)

CRUZ *(on walkie-talkie)*
Come to Stevens. Come to Stevens, we have the cure.
Look for the Amenta to guide you. More information to
come soon.

(Beep)

Come to Stevens. Come to Stevens, we have the cure. Look for the Amenta to guide you. More information to come soon.

> *(Lights down on COLONEL's blank, terrified expression. Beep. Sistrum. End of play.)*

ABOUT THE AUTHOR

David L. Williams is a Phi Beta Kappa graduate of the theatre department of Cornell University, where he was a four time award winner in the Heerman's-McCalmon Playwriting contest. Since then, he has written more than twenty-five plays and musicals in a variety of genres. He is a member of the Dramatist Guild and has won the HotCity Theatre GreenHouse New Play Festival for The Winners, the Riverside Stage Company's Founder's Award for *Ampersand,* and the League of Cincinnati Theatre's best production in the YES Festival award for *Spake.* His work has been produced across the United States and internationally, including the award-winning *The Starving* and *The Wolf Manhood,* along with four selections for the New York International Fringe Festival. He lives in Bellefonte, Pennsylvania with his wonderful wife Kathleen.